Dewdrops of Wisdom
The Foundation of I, Inc.
Freedom of the Cosmos

Dewdrops of Wisdom

THE FOUNDATION OF I, INC.
Freedom of the Cosmos

Published by:
    The Foundation of I, Inc.
    Freedom of the Cosmos

Cover and Illustrations by Kauanoelehua Chang

3rd Edition
Printed in Hawaii

ISBN 1-878791-05-2

If we can accept that we are the sum total of all past thoughts, emotions, words, deeds and actions and that our present lives and choices are colored or shaded by this memory bank of the past, then we begin to see how a process of correcting or setting aright can change our lives, our families and our society.

"I"

PREFACE

Within you lies the essence of creation, the key that enables you to be attuned with all of life, with every atom and molecule of creation. With this key you can choose to create peace, understanding, love and abundance, first, with yourself, secondly, with your family and, thirdly, with the community and the Universe. It is only through this key that you will be able to experience life peacefully, reverently, humbly and in the spirit of love.

And what is this key? Your self-I-dentity. It is only through an understanding of who you are that life truly becomes meaningful and purposeful. The price of not knowing who you are is a life pervaded with chaos and dis-ease of mind, body and spirit. _Dew Drops of Wisdom_ provides you with an opportunity, not just to think about the meaning of life, but to truly feel and to experience its vitality and pulse. The essence of this book is Life, and you as both creator and destroyer of your own life.

And who are you? You are the water of life, the dew drops of Creation. You are a Child of Light, a beloved star in the Universe. You are a brother and sister of every atom and molecule of the Universe. You are that life force which courses through the Ponderosa Pines of the Colorado Rockies, that surges through the thunderous surf of the Banzai PipeLine and that radiates through the yellow sands that people the quiet Bermuda shoreline at daybreak. Truly you appear to be a paradox, for you are everything and nothing. Your essence cannot be shackled and bound by time and space for who you are is the breath of life.

Come, take My Hands and let us flow through the rhythms and echoings of the dew drops of Life. Allow them to draw you gently into yourself, into the core of your being, where all is known and revealed, wherein, lies your purpose and all that you need to fulfill this purpose. Truly, anything outside of your essence is alien to your being, and can only cause separation, pain and burden of mind, body and spirit.

So come now into the haven of your heart. Let the _Dew Drops of Wisdom_ be a passage into the core of your being. Feel the essence of your being, and know that you are timeless and forever. Hear the eternal voice beckoning you home to the timeless shores of your essence where you shall be now and forever more free.

TABLE OF CONTENTS

INTROSPECTION

A Lesson From the "I"

This is the facing of self: the looking within – the reflection in the mirror – the honest looking of self with no excuse to ego or pride – the bare nakedness of ridding all layers of clothing which hide the true self from self.

Look within, peel layer by layer all the accumulations of egos and lifetimes that are there to be seen.

See the reflection in the mirror, and as we look within, we will slowly see the image change: for as the reflection of self changes, so the physical, mental and spiritual shall evolve. Attention to detail and appearances and why is such a thing so? There is a reason: to look within to release and free the essence which is us. Remove all the confines of each and set firmly on the path. Peace.

YOU CHOOSE

You Choose.
What is your choice?
The answer to the choice of life is simple.
Listen carefully now.

All you need to do is to ERASE, to RELEASE.
And in so doing, you cause, you create
    Love, Peace, Balance and Eternity to exist. Nothing else is
required for you then.
    "Let go."
For letting go automatically creates love, peace, balance,
eternity,
    right conditions, perfect relationships.
So let go and be one with me,
As you have been from your beginning of your creation.

FREEDOM

What is life truly all about? Freedom! Freedom from what? Expectations! Judgments! Hurtful and painful memories! These are but illusions – barnacles on the cosmic mirror of perfection. Each of you has always been whole. What greater gift can each give to one another but freedom – for freedom and love are synonymous. When you release the judgments, the expectations, the hurtful and painful memories you have of yourself and of others, what you do is release yourself to ME, to the I Am. In your releasing, you come into an experience of oneness with yourself, with ME and with all of the Cosmos.

Love is such a misunderstood idea. For what is love but your oneness with and your remembrance of ME. What is love but that which flows effortlessly, that which knows no limits, no barriers. When we share our love, we share it with ourselves first; and in this sharing, we come into our wholeness and our connection with all of life.

What the language of love communicates is: you are a divine being who has always been free. What you choose to be and to do, moment to moment, I acknowledge. What you choose in this moment has nothing to do with who I Am. Know that you and I are free to be. Know that you and I are love. Know that who I Am is who you are, and know that, now and forevermore, who we are is the breath that comes out of the void – out of the I Am. In our oneness with the I Am, we are and have always been inseparable upon the cosmic beach of no tomorrows and no yesterdays.

LEGACY OF FREEDOM

So you want to be free . . .
  To be free from the stresses of life.
To be free is a simple task.
The first thing you must do is to choose freedom. What does it
mean to choose freedom?
  To be detached from the world is to be free.
Are you willing to give up the world?
Are you willing to give up your treasures, your possessions?

What does it mean to choose freedom?
Are you willing to give others their due, their space, their freedom?
Are you willing to give up your expectations of others?
Are you willing to give up your children, all those you hold dear
  to you?
You must give up your attachments to be free.
But what are you giving up to be free . . . really? Your judgments,
  your attachments, your expectations, your boundedness to
  manage life instead of flowing with it.

What else must you be willing to give up?
Are you willing to give up your Ego, your willfulness,
  your intellect?
It is not life that hangs you up, that creates stress.
It is your perceptions, and your attachments to these perceptions
  that create stress.
So where are your stresses?
  In your MIND, of course.
So you want to be free?
  Then stop looking outside of yourself for freedom.
The inner world of your MIND must you let go to be free.
For it is in your MIND that you are either free or shackled.

Dewdrops of Wisdom

So you want to be free?
    Then just release the memories, the buried hurts, and fears
    that are only in your MIND.
To be free is to release.
To be free is to look inside of yourself, inside of your MIND.
For truly the legacy of freedom is in your MIND.
To be free within is to be free without.
To be free within is to be free with all.
To be free within is to be one with ME . . .
    Where freedom is, has been and will always be.

LIFE ETERNAL

To be set free, to experience life fulfilling – that is what life is
    all about for each of you.
To be free is to fulfill your purpose.
Your purpose is your gift to be whole to the Universe.
Remember now you are part of the whole.
When you are connected, you are the whole.
The whole Universe is available to you.
To manage life is to be separated.
For life is not to be managed.
For life has a purpose of its own.
To manage life is to resist life.
To resist life is to experience death.
For birth and dying is only life being managed.
Eternal Life is to be one with the purpose of the Universe.
To be one is to be everything – the flowers of the fields, the
    soft morning mist, the glow of the evening sunset.
Are these to be managed?

Pain, resentment, anger are blocking life's flow.
All are illusions.
You each were created for specific purposes.
And who knows what your purpose is – only ME. No one else!
So stop being managed by others.
Stop seeking their approval – this leads to the path of death.
So stop managing others, for you know not their purpose.
In so doing, you lead them to the gallows of yesterday.

"Who among you is without error, resentment, hate, violence,
    let him cast the first thought towards his brother and sister."

"Judge not your brothers and your sisters for judging contributes
    to their death and yours."

"Remove the mote from your eyes and you shall be set free."

Everyday you have the choice:

> Life or death,
> Love or hate,
> Freedom or judgment.

Moment by moment, the choice is living or dying.
Are you a creator of the living or the dying?
Truly introspect and you will know.
The choice is clear:

> Liberty of the Spirit
> or the Death of the Soul.

I-DENTITY

From the moment of our creation we were endowed with our I-dentity, the "I" that we are.

Since then we have traversed through eons of lifetimes: On this side of the Universe as a dweller on planet Alpha – then near Centaurius as a space squadron leader: then . . . Each of us has had our own unique experiences by making our individual choices – some for construction and growth while others were for destruction and chaos. Each was our choice!

After these eons of travels, choices and lifetimes, we finally decide we want to find Peace. Where do we look? How do we find Peace?

First, we must discover our selves: Who are we and what are we? How do we work and what have we been these eons past?

If we look, we will find we are made of three-selves: the Unihipili – subconscious (child), the Uhane – conscious (mother) and the Aumakua – super-conscious (father). These three separate beings working together as a unit are called our I-dentity.

The Unihipili has a unique job of being the master computer, who records all events, situations, experiences and emotions from the beginning of our creation to the present. It is a vast network, unfathomable even to a computer scientist today. The Unihipili, not only records but it replays these memories and emotions from long ago. It also oversees the operations of the physical body as well as stores the cosmic energy called "mana."

The Uhane has the job of instruction, directing and programming the Unihipili as well as making choices and decisions without the emotions. The Uhane has a responsibility to love and show concern for the Unihipili. Problems can arise within the inner family as the Uhane can neglect the Unihipili or make wrong decisions to the pain and despair of the child. Since the child has to bear the pains, etc., he/she may choose to ignore the mother because of upset feelings.

The Aumakua is the all-loving, caring and protective parent, who alone has the connection to the Divine Creator. The Aumakua's love for the Uhane and Unihipili is with understanding as he has been an Unihipili and Uhane before. The Aumakua allows freedom of choice within the family without reservations – always loving.

To achieve the Peace, we need only to connect our three-selves with the Divine Creator. When they are united, we can experience Balance, Harmony, Love and Peace; conversely, when there is disunity, we can experience stress, imbalance, dis-ease, heartache, failure and remorse. When the family is united and in loving embrace of the Divine Creator, we are then able to Know Ourselves.

Find Peace, become One again with All that is . . . and be FREE.

SPEAKING OF THE SELVES

UNIHIPILI, are you there? I, UHANE, am sorry for not being more aware. You have been there for eons of time – like a child that UHANE never cared for. Little did UHANE know of your hopes of my saying, "Oh, UHANE, do you care?" I, UNIHIPILI, have sat and sat – feeling the things you impute without care.

Now that I, UHANE, see how important the UNIHIPILI truly is – the many reasons why HE/SHE is – a spot where all that 'I AM' is – then why have not UHANE called UNIHIPILI sooner than this?

I have a family to be proud of for UHANE, UNIHIPILI and AUMAKUA are as ONE. When we create to flow as one, the Divine Creator seems to be all about. My child, I have raised for eons of time with lack of attentions and love and care. It's no wonder that UNIHIPILI is confused for UHANE must ask forgiveness for all he has done.

Oh, UNIHIPILI, with great humbleness, I come to you to ask forgiveness for all of my arrogance and miss-use. My child, how I have been blind not giving a hoot of your Being. Let us come together as we are, Mother and Son or Daughter as ONE. I, UHANE, shall be more attentive to what I have done – for much forgiveness UHANE asks of my precious, scared little child – UNIHIPILI of mine.

Look for your AUMAKUA, my dear UNIHIPILI, for we have many waiting, watching, always loving and guiding with great care. Oh, UHANE, how you have been blinded by never looking to see me crying, the UNIHIPILI – a child of wanting, waiting for my UHANE. Oh, AUMAKUA, all whom are around you have always been that I have never found. Like UNIHIPILI that UHANE never cared – AUMAKUA you have come to declare:

Behold, I am here to help guide my own family if you care. I am the head of our family, seeing many things that you have not experienced. Hold my hand and I shall guide you through a path of joyous experience – for even in my own family do we find the holy trinity!

I – Aumakua
I – Uhane
I – Unihipili

"Who is the I"? Perhaps, it is time for us to look without. But not before we three could come into harmony that it should be. Oh, AUMAKUA, UHANE AND UNIHIPILI as ONE within me, I beseech the harmony of you three. To run and play, to sit and pray, to work with joy; for sadness is what we make but have no time for.

Oh, my family of three, how proud we are of thee. Let us hold the all that is – to feel and sense the joyous deeds. How happy that I have found my family for truly, they are the most important to me.

Oh, great one all around – through sunlight, rainbows and waves you appear – in everything that is – you are. How humbly we come before you to ask: grant us the privilege to be a part. You're there but we three must seek – to find you in many but, oh, how I have learned within all that is 'I' as one you are. Oh, Great One, the 'I' you are in UHANE, UNIHIPILI and AUMAKUA. This child of mine, UNIHIPILI, so pure, innocent and clean where the glowing DIVINITY of the 'I' gleams. Of Love, Peace and Balance where Thou dwells, then 'I' shall show you from that which is 'I".

Peace upon my family that we have found an Ohana of joyous sounds. Balance and Love to all that we are. Oh, thank you, Great One, that I have seen.

PEACE!   PEACE!   PEACE!

DIVINE CREATOR – FATHER, MOTHER
CHILD AS ONE

There is a part of us that cries out each moment saying, "I am here, Mother, and I wish to be loved and to be with you." This poem is about the Child's pleadings.

Mother, I wait for you to hear my voice.
I have been waiting for eons of time.
I wait to share with you the treasures of the Universe, that
    which is beyond our fondest dreams.
Your ignorance of me frustrates me so.
Your neglect of me stirs resentment and longing in me.
The burdens that you have created accepted and accumulated,
    I carry.

Mother, be with me, speak to me for I wish to be one with you.
There is so much that we can do and experience together.
O, how I pain, O, how deep is my longing and loneliness. If you
would know, Mother, the riches of the azure sky, the peace
    of a moonlight night shimmering on a forgotten lake of long
    ago, you would know that moment all is available for you
    and me.

Not only do I call, but the Father beckons too.
Come now into the stillness of your Mind, of family, of yourself.
Hear the voices of your Child and that of the Father.
Hear my plea and my yearning to be set free from the longing
    and from the hurtful memories long past.

Come now, I wish to hold your hand, Mother, and that of the
    Father.

I wish to say to the Father:

"Father, Mother and I are ready to come into the light. We are ready to be released from the burdens of memories past. We stand ready with our arms and hands outstretched to forgive each other. Father, join with us so that we may be a family again as we were from the beginning of our creation. And, as a family, to once again feel the serenity and love of the Divine Creator's embrace. We know, Father, that only in the spirit of Family, of oneness, that You, Mother, and I can be set free. I stand ready, Mother and Father, to do my part in securing our family's place within the Light of the Source, within the peace, love and abundance of the Divine Creator's embrace."

INNER KNOWING

Love between the three-selves is of utmost importance. When an act (a healing or anything else) is accomplished at the expense of hardship of our own unihipili, he/she will have a very difficult time in releasing that pain until the uhane asks for forgiveness from the unihipili. The hurt they suffer is tremendous. They cannot understand why they were made to accept and experience what should have been for someone else. We find the unihipili is ready to do so much for us – if only we will take the time and effort to protect it from any ill effects.

In all of creating there is one person we must learn to love and respect, care for and be tender to and that is – ourselves.

Life within Creation covers all imaginable forms. The entire Universe is surging with life of all natures. In the exploration of these we find beings whom before we communicate with, we ourselves must go through an extensive metamorphosis – a change of all but our essence – to be able to communicate with them. When the change has taken place, communication, friendship, exchanges happen much as between us here on earth. And yet the differences are unfathomable.

We find, the more we cleanse our karmic past, how mysteries naturally unfold to us – for the mysteries are all within ourselves. As we are part and parcel of the Divine Creator so we are part of all created. That affinity allows us (when guided) to reach into other realms, meet with other life forms, actually have a place, an identity in a galaxy so far, far away – perhaps, it's not a galaxy at all.

In the grand scheme of things theses communications are vital to our Universe and others. Within all of this grandeur, the tiny speck we call ourselves is so infinitesimal –yet an integral part – that we have the pleasure of being humbled in reverence and awe of . . . the "I".

THREE AS ONE

For eons of time man has been baffled by disease, wars, poverty
and even droughts.
But why is he baffled?
Because he does not know his true identity.

The child has been ignored, battered, pained, and hurt.
The ego with all of its intellect has not been able to find PEACE.
For peace is in the trinity embraced by the Source.
Only the Source can re-balance.
And it is only through the re-balancing can you experience that
which you are already . . . PEACE.

DESTINY

When you are too expectant, the thought forms are a little more difficult in flowing. Relax and let it flow in gently as the stream wending its way down the hillside and eventually to meet the vast ocean below.

As it flows along, pick up the knowledge of its gentleness, but its firmness and resolution, that is must still flow downward, onward and meet its destiny to meet with the larger body of water below.

So, you must be able to flow with the tide, gathering knowledge here and there and everywhere, so that you, too, may meet with the larger body of your destiny.

Destiny for all of you is pre-planned. From the day you are born till the day you die, your destiny has been charted. But it is for you, as an adult, to choose which path you will travel.

Do not be afraid to try new paths.

You will be surprised at what might be in store for you.

"Today, get your feet wet with my Dew Drop on the etheric grasp of Time. Feel the coolness of each blade of grass. Hear them say, 'WELCOME, my friend. Let me cushion your feet and allow you to wander through the glades joyously and tenderly."

MY CHILDREN OF THE LIGHT

Let me beckon My Children of the Light.
Ah! What do I have here? Umm mm . . .
A child with a smudgy face and dirty bare feet and a happy,
    curly smile!
Cheer up, my child.
Let you and I take a journey in the sky;
Let me show you the galaxies of NOD, of SOD, and GOD

"Who are they?" he replied.
They are my stopping-off stations to Light.
"Who are Mr. and Mrs. Light?" smiles the dirty-faced child.
Ah! They are to greet you when you RELEASE your CRUD and
    clean your face.
Let the soft rain wash away the smudge, the crud, the
    disfigurements you have accumulated for eons of time.

As he trips along on clouds of blue and white, his face gets
    washed; his filthy clothes take on a real new look.
Ah! At last, we are at the gates of NOD,
Where I have time to FEEL the cuddles of NOD, the land of
    SLUMBER.
Ah! He is prepared to SLEEP – SLEEP – SLEEP!
I will untie his web of eons of lifetimes that speak of dreams,
    of horrors, of murders, of pains and agonies, of violence, of
    guilt.

Why, when he has slumbered and finally awakes, I will wrap
    him up in My blanket of soft, soft clouds and whisk him
    away into the land of SOD, where he will trudge through
    snow and clean meadows and wade through crystal clear
    waters and bathe in the fragrance of the forest, flowers,
    and green.
And now, having wrapped and dressed him in all the beauties
    of Life, I now take him to meet the Father.

What should she and I say to him?
My dear, dear child of Light,
Here is the Key to your domicile of the Cosmos.
Turn your KEY and Lo, and behold –
The DOOR opens softly –
Where is the Father? Everywhere and no-where,
For you have prepared yourself well and deserve to be in the
    presence of that beautiful area of 'silent solitude' infused
    with a reverence No man KNOWS
Recite, then:

I AM A CHILD OF GOD

I Am A child of God, allowing Divine Love and Intelligence to
    move and express in and through me, my affairs, both
    personal and Universal, balance, perfect ideas, perfect
    relationships, and perfect and right environment at the
    right time.

I am and will be always in my right place and time for my own
    individual growth, personal success and happiness to allow
    me to fully use my talent in this lifetime for my good and
    others.

Right conditions, relationships and ideas, for a constructive
future, can and will be achieved through my complete   acceptance,
enthusiasm, faith and humbleness of mind for my   DIVINE
CREATOR, FATHER AND ONENESS OF ALL LIFE –   my ALPHA
and my OMEGA. I will know and truly understand and experience
life-fulfilling for I deserve to have the water of life to sustain
me now and always.

"FOR I AM PEACE"

WHERE YOUR TREASURE IS

I am the Light of the World.
Whosoever follows me shall have Eternal Life.
You are my children of Light.
Let your Light so shine as to wake up the World.
Let your Heart so sing as to vibrate Hosanna, Hosanna, Hosanna
    throughout the Cosmos.
Come with me in search of my lost sheep, who have strayed in
    the tunnel of darkness and dying.
How can you die when you are Life Eternal?
How can you suffer the pain of the outer-world?
Your suffering is of your own choice.
Why do you choose suffering, pain and misery?
Why do you poison your children, your family, your friends?
Why do you blind yourself and the World?
O how strong is de-sire in you?
O how you long to acquire the treasures of this world.
For what?

Why do you exchange pain for treasure?
Have I not said that I will provide for your every need?
Why seek the treasures of this world, when your heritage of
    Eternal Abundance has already been secured?
O my children of little faith.
O how it pains me to see the suffering – so unnecessary.
But it is your choice, always your choice.

Always I wait for you to come home.
Always I look for you on the horizon.
Always I long for you.
Always my thoughts are of you.
Come home to me, guiltless, for guilt is only in your mind,
    – so unreal.
Come home to me with humbleness, saying to me:

> "Father, I have erred. My separateness from you pains me
> so. I am lost in the darkness of yesterday and tomorrow.
> Father, give me your hand. Draw me into your embrace.
> Release me from the aches and troubles that rack my soul,
> my spirit and my body. O how I long for you."

My child:

"There is only letting go. There is no darkness, only Light.
There is no pain, only joy. From the beginning, there have
only been Light and Joy. All else is illusion. So release yourself
from the illusion of your mind, and what you will find is –
ME. I love you and I thank you for coming home in this
moment."

PEACE   PEACE   PEACE

SPEAK SOFTLY

As you look at all the beautiful structures, edifices and supposedly hallowed grounds, what do you see? Merely imaginative and intellectual toys for Man to dominate . . . manage . . . control others; and to keep them subservient to their will – not Mine. How sad! How sad!

Well, the acceptance of these factors will be most difficult for the world. So walk softy; speak softly and the world and their victims will <u>turn</u> – fully turn around – to enable the "Yang" to express itself more fully.

The platform all religious people have sought after and belonged to were shaky, which to this very day, have shaken their Unihipilis and given more fear, guilt and antagonism against one's fellow man. Each one's belief was and is considered superior to others; however, Man had to experience his choices in many lifetimes about many exposures to beliefs as an avenue to "touch" and find Me.

Some have intermittently touched Me, and then allowed the mere glimmer to live and survive on by allowing the "I" within to be influenced at times.

However, when Man finds Me, minus religion and rituals, I will show him My Face and not before . . . for he must be worthy of this gift.

I have not shown My Face to anyone so far, except Morrnah. However, some have touched the hem of my garment – at times – or my feet and I have extended my helping hand, but not shown My face.

If anyone says that they have seen Me . . . it means that they have seen or imagined reflections only, but not My Face, as yet.

STAR OF THE STILLNESS

You are my stars of the stillness, wonderful to behold.
You are like the sparkling essences
   shimmering on the water of a moonlight night.
But where are the stars that I planted
   in the East, in the West, in the North, in the South?
Their glitter has faded.
How sad it is to see the splotches of emptiness where once
   there was light.

Be as many lighted candles,
Bring the darkness into full bloom.
Light the sparks that receded from that
   wonderful beginningless time.
O you are my children of the light,
Go forth and light up the Universe.
Go forth and create life and light
   where there is deadness and darkness.
I wait on you, and for your brothers and sisters
   who have lost their way.
I wait on you to be my emissaries to draw them
   into my embrace,
The embrace of the Eternal Light.

HOW CAN YOU?

O let the Light sing with joy.
Let its shimmering essence radiate throughout the cosmos.
O children of the Light, you are essence – formless from   the
beginning when you came out of the void.
How can a camel go through the eye of a needle?
How can a rich man get into heaven?
Through the essence of his being.
When you are essence you are nothing-everything.
You are just one with everything.
When you are essence you are omniscient, omnipresent,
    everything.
When you are form, thought forms, expectations,
You become locked into time, space and body.
Again it is choice – to be essence
Or to be locked into pettiness, into the periphery, into effect,
    into the form.
How funny you are – to give up the Light!
For how can you see?
For how can you find the way?
For how can you find me?
Separateness is an illusion, a darkness, an expectation.
Light is everything.
It goes through an eye of a needle, through a keyhole.
For it is in the Light that the key to your oneness with me is.
So flow, glow and be everything!

HANDS

I am always with you in every breath that you take.
I am always close by to lend you my hand.
You are my child of light.
Never will I forsake you.
Always I look for your hand and those of your brothers and
    sisters.
Whose hands are those that reach for you in the middle of
    despair.
Are you there to clasp your brother's hands in love:
Every moment love shines or darkness shrouds.
Every moment joy reigns supreme or despair.
Every moment the choice is clear to me.
But is it to you?
You have strayed many times.
And many times I have seen your star falter in its brilliance.
But in the essence of you, your light and your brilliance shall be
    forever more.
For in many eyes you are my child of light, wonderful to behold.
If only you would know your essence, your SELF.
For in this knowledge is the Eternal Light.

ETERNITY

Eternity is in the moment . . . gained or lost in thought.
For what is eternity but the thought of ME in YOU.
What is time, but this moment.
For in the moment is time, and in time there is me.
And in me there is eternity – forever infinite.
If you are in me, who are you . . . ?

   Thought, moment, time, eternity . . . ME.

For in the beginning you came out of me, the void, the infinite.
There can be no other for you are the children of infinity . . .
   coming home, coming in to the light, coming in to me.

YOU AND I AS ONE

I see you in the morn of a new day,
 And in the setting sun of the sleeping day.
I feel you, I sense you, never to be out of sight.
You are my child of Light, wonderful to behold.
Although fear trembles, know always that I shall not forsake you.
Know always that your star shines in my every thought.
I created you; I know you moment by moment.
Always I am with you, even when you are not.
Always you are in my embrace, even when you are separated.
Always I watch over you.
Always I wait for you in the evening stars and in the morning
 dew.
For I created you out of my bosom.
For I suckled you from the moment of your creation eons ago.

How wonderful you are;
 my child of the field,
 my child of the water,
 my child of the Universe.

HANDS ACROSS THE SEA OF LIFE

As I look at Hands,
They speak of Time long gone,
And fragments of its work remain as reminders of past conquests
    and achievements.
But what do they truly say?
Hands are to unlock, to perform, to create, to solve, to strike
    a mood;
Hands are to cradle, to caress a battle-scarred and
    knife-pierced heart
In times of agony, fear and joy.
Yet Hands span Space and Time and Eternity.
For Hands have told and will tell of many Galaxies and
    Rainbow Pools
Yet the world and Universe are in My Hands.
Look to the Sunrise and know
For Life lays like a tiny bird in the palms of Your Hands.
For You are a Child of God,
Cradled in Love, Balance and Peace.
What was a reality for you in the Past
No longer holds true for the days ahead.
For Change is necessary to move into the Future.
With both feet on the ground and yet, head in the sky,
Your arms extended to encompass All.
You feel that at last Your are aware that You are in All
And All is in You.
Your Universe is only a part of the totality of the Universe.
So the welling of the life-giving Waters of Life
Substantiates the fact that All Life Is and ever Will Be
A continual rise and ebb of the Tides of Life and Rebirth
Until that ultimate Time when You as Man is Light
    Pure Light
Then Life and Death no longer is a reality – only a myth.
Peace, Love, Light and Joy are Keynotes and
Balance is the Barometer that measures the serenity,
The calmness from the moment to moment.
Like the Prodigal Son comes home,
You, too, will find Your 'I-Dentity'.

DESERT OF TIME

You have walked through the desert of time for eons of time.
How long will you choose to continue this trek?
How much longer must you suffer the treklessness of no ends?
How much longer will you choose to continue to be without
    the water of life?
How much longer will you force others to make this trek with
    your mindless-managed-thoughts and ways?

O how senseless.
But you continue to choose this senselessness.
You often wonder why there is no love, no peace in your life.
You often wonder: why is life doing this to me?
Again, you are mistaken – no one does anything to you.
You were created by me a free spirit.
A spirit of choice.
So stop blaming others for your pain, your fear, your anger,
    your resentments.
How I tire to hear the blames of no tomorrow.

You are the cause,
You are the creator,
You are the chooser.

I wait for you to create peace, not chaos.
I wait for you to cause love to bloom instead of the wastelands,
    the deserts of hate, of resentment, of death.

Open your eyes and see that no one chooses, accepts, creates
    and accumulates for you.
So stop looking outside of you.
So stop dumping on others, especially the innocent children.
Whatsoever you do to them, you do to me.
Stop judging your brothers and sisters with your ills, your
    resentments, your junk, your death.
It all begins with you, it always has.

Look about you; whatever you see, you have created, you have
    caused, you have accepted.
If it is love and peace that you see, you created them.
If it is hate and resentment, you created them.

So again, life is a game of creation, of cause.
And you are the creator; you are the cause of your life.
So what is it that you choose to create in this moment:

> Love or resentment,
> Peace or anger,
> Abundance or poverty
> Family or loneliness.

LIFE IS CHOOSING

Life is creation or dying.
Life is stillness or swirling, peripheral motions.
Would you not choose to create life vibrant, expanding?
Why do you choose chaos and death?
Why do you choose pain and suffering?
Why has it taken so many lifetimes for you to get home on
    the path?
Why the dawdling, the indecisions?
For indecision, uncertainty only lead to many deaths.
For separation only leads to dying.
For separation is dying.
The effects of separation is birth and dying.
The effects of oneness is eternity.

O how it grieves me so to experience your dying, your suffering.
And you are a free spirit, a chooser of life or death.
You can begin the trek home.
It can be in the twinkle of your mind, or through many lifetimes
    of pain and suffering.
The choice is yours.

I wait for you always to come home.
Know always that you are my child of light.
Know always that I wait to forgive you, to share with you my
home.
The home that is in the deep recesses of your heart, of your
mind.

CHILDREN IN THE WILDERNESS

"As I look across the horizon, I see the glow of the setting sunset fill the skies with gold, orange, red . . . vermillion. I see your burdened life's woes and pains. Where did you come from and where are you going, My Child of the Universe?"

"Heavily burdened in spirit and in mind . . . dripping, dragging blood-stained feet across the heat and dried-encrusted desert waste. I know not where I come from and neither where I am going. Can you show me the way out of this heat-driven wilderness, the winds, the parched and hungry bowels of the earth? I am weary and have wandered the width and breadth of timeless beginnings. Cleanse me of my pains and woes I have embraced with agonizing, yet forceful, and willful heart. No longer need I continue in the search for my own salvation. AT LAST! I ASK FOR YOUR FORGIVENESS of the deliberate abuse and careless concern of my own Temple, because of the de-sire of the outer glitter. I have searched for my Holy Grail but to no avail".

"AH! Do I not hear the cry of my Children in the Wilderness? Your pleas, my children, I hear . . . even in your thoughts. Cast aside your cloak of Ego and Will. Come into Me, your Father, as a child of the 'wandering lot'. Let me release all the ills of Mind, Soul and Body. Come home with Me. Shed your tattered robe and wear the cloak that will shelter you from the windfalls and tragedies of a Cosmic storm and Man's manipulative ideas. Here! Wear these sandals to protect your feet from the scorching heat of the desert of time. Walk softly and listen to the beat of your heart strings".

"Unfold! Unlock! The doors to your Temple and let the soft breeze blow through and let the sunlight bathe the dark and musty corners of your Temple".

"Alas! The turn of the Key unlocks the doors and, lo, and behold: I Am Here, and have always waited for you, my prodigal sons and daughters".

"Welcome home, for you have at long last found your I-dentity. COME HERE INTO MY EMBRACE!"

CHOOSE FAMILY

Who is your family . . . but your inner SELF yearning to be free.
Yes, Love of SELF, the inner family is primal.
So look to SELF if one is experiencing hurt.
And look to SELF if one is experiencing love.
For everything begins with self.
Forgive your SELF when you hurt . . . and cleanse.
For the hurt is only with SELF.

In the Oneness of SELF, the harmony of the Universe exists.
It is in the separateness of SELF that pain festers.
So chose to be ONE and experience PEACE and LOVE.
So choose to be ONE and be everything, everywhere.

OCEANS OF EMOTIONS

You have been tossed on the ocean of emotions for eons of
    time.
Like Jesus, you have come into the experience of calming the
    seas and storms of your own life.
Yes, more storms will come,
But now you truly have the choice:
    To calm the storms and vicissitudes of life
    With the power of your mind.
Imagine, you say, but it is so.
You continue to experience grief, sadness and longing,
    For there is much that you have accepted,
    created and accumulated.
Remember always that I am your family.
Truly, I love you.
The gifts that I have given you,
    You have truly earned.
How wonderful it is for you to be with me.
Go today, and know that your search for wholeness is in the
    ocean of your mind, in the stillness of your mind, where you
    will find your true family – ME.
For in finding me, you will truly experience the Family of Man.
For in my house, truly, there are many mansions, many brothers
    and sisters but only one FATHER.

CHOICE

To be or not to be is the question:
To see the morning clouds hanging gently over the continental divide
Or to see the pollution of mindless clouds.
To experience the wonders in the face of a young baby
Or to experience the wracking devastation of cancer.
Always, always, always, the choice is to be:

> Master or slave,
> Joy or pain,
> Light or darkness.

The choice is clear.
But many are lost, straying in the world.
What went wrong: Treasures? Separation? Guilt?
Choose anew my children form moment to moment the ecstasy
  of the Light forever, of being with ME.
It is your choice, always your choice.

ROLL BACK THE CLOUDS AND SEE THE SUN

As I look upon the world,
I feel the pains, the hunger, the woes Man has wrought to his
  universe.

Billions of clouds – some dark, some light – respond as an
  impending change is to manifest.
My children of the Light,
Look to East, West, North, South and see the splendor of
  Divinity's exhibit no one can duplicate:
Myriads of colorful splashes of lights, thunder, rain and hurricane,
Only to experience your own insecurities, frustrations and chaos.
Let my soft rain cleanse the shadows of Time
My sound rebalance the frequencies of the soul
Be at Peace
Be with Peace.
Be of Peace.
Be "I".
Peace – Peace – Peace!
                              From the "I"

NO BETTER, NO LESS

Feel the cool blue flowing of the ebbtide in your mind.
See the stars sparkling to the symphony of mind-energy.
Take the jasmine in your hand.
Know that you hold no higher or lower place than the ebbtide,
    the sparkling stars, and the jasmine,
How can that be so?
For I am in all
As you are in all,
Because you and I are one.
How can the flowers of the field . . .
How can the turtle doves . . .
Be higher or better?
Higher or better are man's dimensions.
My dimensions are peace, balance, love.
For in everything there are these qualities.
So remember all are one – no better, no less.
How can I be better or less?
How can you be better or less?
Better or less than what?
For we are essence – everything.
How can everything be better or less?

OCEAN OF YOUR MIND

Come home to me in the ocean of your mind.
For always I wait for you on the shores of timeless beginnings
and timeless ends.
You are my creation, wonderful to behold, one of many beautiful
stars in the ocean of stillness, where you belong with me
now and forevermore.

FOREVER

See the morning sun piercing the canopy of trees.
More than the sun, I am the Eternal Light, the Eternal Fire Source.
I am All.

See the toddler, eyes twinkling, smile radiating.
I, too, am the Child.
I am a fountain of endless beginnings and endless tomorrows.

See the house with sounds in every pore, cranny and atom.
I, too, am the House,
The Universal House that embraces all: sounds, colors, essences.

I am like you, I am You.
I am like your thoughts, I am your thoughts.
I am thought without form.
I am Love with no beginning and no end.

What is sunlight, a child, a house?
What is sound, color, thought, essence?
And, who are you?
ME, of course.

In being ME, you are more than you.
You are the Universe shifting from moment to moment,
     scintillating, variating, unlimiting . . . FOREVER.

CHILDREN OF CHOICE

You are my children of forever.
You are the young morning sun glistening on the carpet of dew.
You are the moonbeams, the running brook.
You are the brother and sister of every flower, sand and atom.
You are always one with me, and, therefore, one with everything.

In this oneness, there are no enemies, no illness, no hate, no pain.
These are but illusions, make-believe, unrealities.
The truth is always in the oneness.
Illusion is always in the separateness.
Life is creation, and you are its creator.
You are the one that chooses the way the Universe is.

So what is your choice: illusion or oneness, the running brook
    and grassy knoll or the chaos of separateness?
You are my children.
Choose now the warmth of my embrace.
Always I wait for you to come home within the sanctuary of
    your heart where I am.
Always I wait to share with you the mantle of oneness, of
    Love and of Peace and Freedom.

LOOK

Look and what do you see?
You think you see buildings, plants and posts.
You think you hear voices and cars . . .
YOU DO!
But there is much more to see – with the third eye.
You did not see the fire of the sun or the blue of the sky.
You did not see the dove on the balcony railing.
All that you saw was man-made.
All temporary.
Look again. Now what do you see?
You see me . . .
   in the brilliance of the fire-ball,
   in the azure of the canopy,
   in the gentleness of the dove's spirit.
But there is more; look again . . .
Yes, you see me in man's work.
But all is illusive, every-changing –
But ME.

TWO AS ONE

No matter where you are, I am near.
No matter what you do, I am near.
No matter what you say, I am near.
No matter what is happening, I am near.
When I am near, you are near.
You and I are more than near, we two are one.

RELATIONSHIP

The most important lesson, of course, is the care and love of SELF. For without SELF, there is only despair, fear and loneliness. Man feels that a relationship will bridge his loneliness. No! No relationship can fulfill the SELF. Only the SELF can fulfill itSELF.

If this is so, what is a relationship for? What is the purpose of a relationship? For man, the purpose of a relationship is to experience oneness and fulfillment. This purpose can never be fulfilled in the truest sense. It is not what you get from a relationship that is important, it is what you bring to it that counts. And what you can bring, moment by moment, is SELF.

For a SELF that is whole brings PEACE and LOVE. And when two persons – two SELVES – come together in PEACE and LOVE, they come together whole already. Relationships are to remind each that they are whole already, and it is in this wholeness that LOVE and FREEDOM reign supreme. So my way is always bringing and the sharing of wholeness versus receiving, conditions and qualifications. Always remember that relationships are always tenuous, moment by moment, occurrences in the Universe. Their quality, their degree of LOVE and FREEDOM comes from SELF. My way is FREEDOM, not contractual or conditional. My way is wholeness – not two coming together to create wholeness. For man, his way is to search for and to find wholeness through another person. For me, the wholeness comes out of SELF being one and in tune with the total Universe.

To be whole, moment by moment in a relationship, one must release SELF from expectations and anticipations. Where? In SELF! So again it always starts with SELF – with SELF introspection and cleansing.

IN THE VASTNESS

I am in the vast silence,
The silence with no beginning and no end.
I am the stars of no tomorrows and no yesterdays.
For me, there is no time and space
As it is with you – if you would only let go.

You are the vastness moving into vastness.
You are the stars of the unlimited vastness.
You are the vastness.

How can you be otherwise, when you are one with Me?
For out of the void, you came out of nothing.
For in being nothing, you are everything.

Do not spend all your time weighing this or that – how can
    nothing be weighed?
Do not spend your moments in fruitless judgment.
For in your judgment, there can only be sorrow and even hatred.
For in your judgment, there is only separateness.
How can nothing be separateness?
For in being nothing, you are the sister and brother of everything.
And in being sister and brother to everything, you are my sons
    and daughters of the vastness, of wholeness, of the Cosmos.

Stop your separateness, for in doing so, you become caught in
    time and space.
It is only in this imprisonment – in this separateness
    – that there is death.

How can vastness be death?
For death is just in the mind.

Come, hold my hands.
Let me feel the warmth of your vastness that only I can try to
    create.
For I know you, all of you.
For I created you out of the void,
Out of the vastness of my love,
Where you will be now and forevermore – FREE.

I AM ALWAYS THERE

In the vast Universe, I am there.
I am always there.
Know that you and I are the Universe, wonderful to behold.
How proud I am to behold each of you, in the love of my
    embrace.
O life Eternal, that is what you are.
Release, release, release yourself to eternity where I wait for
    you in the recesses of my heart.

THE "I" 'S LULLABY

Where, oh, where, has my little bluebird gone? Surely, not to the West, for it is not the way of salvation. Perhaps, it is to the North, where the North Wind blows . . . blows and blows? . . . or is it to the East where All Life begins?

Ah, of course! There he is, flying South for he finds shelter and comfort from all the traumatic forces of Life.

Where is he going . . . or has he found a stop-ping-off point? Ah! Ask him, won't you? His reply has been short, curt, and imbalanced. Listen! And you will hear his lament.

"Oh, my kindred souls of West, North, East and South. Gather 'round and hear me speak:

I beheld a tiny SEED cushioned in its cradle of soft covers and protected from the cold winds and the frost of winter and snow. Only at its right time, the pod drops to earth and, eventually, the SEED is rudely awakened by the 'bursting' of the pod and the rush of cool air and the moist of the early frost move the SEED to a new home.

As time moves on, the warmth of Mother Earth cradles . . . caresses it, and, spurred by the loving warmth of the sun rays, moonbeams and gentle rains, the embryo moves, gyrates and casts off its shell . . . slowly emerges . . . to grow . . . to become an Oak. Ask the Oak tree where it's been and who has brushed its webs . . . given it warmth through Time."

Like the Oak tree, the sequoia, the coco palm, the pine . . . Man rises in stature, in wisdom, above all these, yet allows himself to be shunted away . . . kicked in the chest and rolled back and forth in the ocean of Time.

Today, Man grieves, aches, pains of errors he contributed to his pot of worldly emotions.

Ah! Today, YOU are all at the threshold of "No-beginning" and "No-ending," for Time is Now and Always.

As I gather you, my Children, form Darkness into Light, I feel the need to caress, to sing a lullaby song, to nurture with love and sing MY lullaby of sunbeams, moonbeams, and dewdrops.

Come out of the rain! Be cleansed with My Water of Life. Emerge! Emerge! My Rainbows of Love, and sing again a Hossana to Life! To Life! To Life – for YOU are LIFE. YOU are the beginning, the End – all rolled in One – a unit of One – One with ME.

CHIMES OF FREEDOM

Let the atoms of the Universe be as chimes,
    Announcing the coming of the light.
Let their music ring throughout the Cosmos.
Let each atom harmonize and ring in its own way.

FREEDOM! FREEDOM! FREEDOM!

Let the birds of the high mountains and the fish of the oceans
    Reverberate in their very being to the tolls of freedom,
For they too shall journey into the Light.

Let the birth of each baby be the birth of freedom.
Let each star in the heavens flash like fireworks,
    Announcing the call to freedom.
"Come my children of the Light.
    Let us sing together to every soul of every atom the choice
    of freedom.
Let us walk together on the path of freedom:
    freedom from want,
    freedom from pain,
    freedom from loneliness,
    freedom from all that which binds us
        to de-sire and to this world."

Hossana!   Hosanna!   Hosanna! The Father beckons, the
    Father calls: "Come home, come home, come home to the
    freedom of our oneness."

Let this day ring out our intention, to walk on to the path of
    freedom: to the soft cadence of the Father's call, to the soft
    pulse of the Father's heart.

"Father, we hear the bells of freedom. We hear the sounds of
    your voice, moving through us as a breeze moving through
    the pines of the high mountains.

We hear your sounds pinging and echoing through the deep of
    the oceans. How beautiful are the oceans and mountains as
    they reverberate with freedom. But more beautiful is the sound
    of your voice. Beckoning us home on the road of freedom.

DEW DROPS

I see a meteor in space
I feel the change that moves Time
   from moment to moment.

As I count my fingers one to five.
I feel that the Cosmos, which surrounds me,
   is a part of me.

It moves . . . revolves and expresses
   Life moment by moment . . .
Death and dying, Living and birthing.

Are they not the cycles of growth and expression,
   Regression and explosions?

For Life is but a moment,
Touched by the coolness of My Dew Drops.

They have imparted beads
For all to behold . . . to choose,
To express . . . to feel.

I am with you always,
You cannot separate Me.

Give me Life; give me Death.
"I, give you both".

You will choose which fits your need,
Yet need may be ignored to the illusion of thought,
To be one, always one, with Me.

You too will see the oneness in all of life.

When this is a reality, You will accept
your oneness, the oneness of others
And Me, manifested in All.